Building Jewish Iden

T0152067

PEOPLE OF THE BOOK

OUR SACRED TEXTS

By Judy Dick

BEHRMAN HOUSE
www.behrmanhouse.com

Design: Terry Taylor Studio
Editor: Dena Neusner
Editorial consultants: Ellen J. Rank, Diane Zimmerman

Copyright © 2013 Behrman House, Inc.
Published by Behrman House, Inc.
Springfield, NJ 07081
www.behrmanhouse.com

ISBN: 978-0-87441-865-1
Printed in the United States of America

The publisher wishes to acknowledge the following sources for quotes:
Chagall quote on page 4: Andre Verdet, *Chagall's World; Reflections From the Mediterranean*. Doubleday, 1984
Wasserstein quote on page 4: Judea and Ruth Pearl, ed. *I Am Jewish: Personal Reflections Inspired by the Last Words of Daniel Pearl*, Jewish Lights, 2005
Sharansky quote on page 5: Natan Sharansky, *Fear No Evil*. PublicAffairs, 1998
Heschel quote on page 5: A.J. Heschel, *Moral Grandeur and Spiritual Audacity* (ed. by Susannah Heschel; Farrar Straus & Giroux, 1997)
Quote on page 23: from an interview with the author
Quote on page 36: Abraham J. Heschel, *Between God and Man*. Free Press, 1997

The publisher gratefully acknowledges the following sources of photographs and graphic images:
(T=top, B=bottom, L=left, R=right, M=middle)
Debby Aharon-Levitt: 5MR, 43B; Risa Towbin Aqua 9TR; Art Resource: RMN-Grand Palais 35L, Cameraphoto Arte (Venice) 35 BR; Associated Press: Gino Domenico 4R, 5BR; iStockphoto: nano (cover boy, 25), tovfla (cover scroll), tovfla 14T, ruchela 48; Jewish Reconstructionist Movement (Women's Torah Project) 14B; Doris Krain 22B; Richard Lobell 30B; NASA 45B; Dena Neusner 28T; Ed Weberman courtesy of NACOEJ 23B; Shutterstock: Phish Photography (cover, tablets), Rob Marmion (cover, girl), Jacek Chabraszewski 2, Poznyakov 3, Luba 6L, Vadim Georgiev 6BR, Maxx-Studio 8T, somchaiP 8B and 9, Nicku 10T, James Steidl 10B, heromen30 11T, J. McPhail 11B, saar 12T, marFot 12B, Kiselev Andrey Valerevich 13T, ecco (scroll) 13, Alexander Dvorak (text) 13B, Stavchansky Yakov (writing) 14B, Garsya (quill) 14B, Matt Ragen (scroll) 14B, sweetok (thread) 14B, Mastepanov Pavel (magnifying glass) 15B, Eduard Kyslynskyy 18, trucic 18B, stefanolunardi 19T, Monkey Business Images 19B, Julie Boro 21, Lutya 22T, SeanPavonePhoto 24T, AISPIX by Image Source 24MR, David Ashley 26, Howard Sandler 27T, Orrza 27B, Jacek Chabraszewski 29, IdeaStepConceptStock 30T, Ivaschenko Roman 33, Neamov (background) 33, ravl 34T, Cathy Keifer 34B, jorisvo (Kunsthistorisches Museum, Vienna) 35TR, HelgaLin 36, Neftali 39T, Rob Bouwan 39B, Max Topchii 40B, Juriah Mosin 41T, Mikhail 42B, Ursula 44, MaszaS 45M, Jacek Chabraszewski 47; Tom Verniero (Caldwell, NJ) 5ML, 25B; Wikimedia Commons: Jewish Women's Archive (cover main photo, 1), Jewish Museum, New York (cover dancing), 4ML, 4BL, Kika Sso 5BL, Matson Photo Service (text) 15B, Gustave Doré 16, National Gallery of Art 20, Westend Synagogue, Germany 24ML, Efrat Amano via PikiWiki 24B, Alfredovic 27M, Goodoldpolonius2 28BL, John Rylands Library 28MB, Diaspora Museum Tel Aviv 28BR, DerHexer 31, wiki 32L, F. Wessel 32R, Jewish Museum 35MR, 37, 38TR, 38BL, vlasta2 40T, 43T.

Library of Congress Cataloging-in-Publication Data

Dick, Judy.
  People of the book : our sacred texts / by Judy Dick.
      pages cm. -- (Building Jewish identity ; 3)
  ISBN 978-0-87441-865-1
  1. Judaism--Sacred books--Juvenile literature. 2. Jewish religious education--Textbooks for children. I. Title.
  BM496.6.D53 2013
  296.1--dc23
                        2012047975

To my nieces and nephews, who make the stories in books come alive as we read them together.

—Judy Dick

CONTENTS

CHAPTER 1

LIVING BY THE BOOK

"Its ways are pleasant ways, and all its paths are peaceful. (The Torah) is a tree of life for those who grasp it, and those who uphold it are happy." (Proverbs 3:17-18)

The Torah is called many things in Jewish tradition: a precious gift, the deep sea, a tree of life, an everlasting flame. It offers something for everyone—an inspiration for art and music, movies, and books; the source of wisdom and justice; a guide for living an ethical life. What do you already know about the Torah? What would you like to know?

I have turned for reference to a great, universal book, the Bible. Since childhood . . . it inspired me in my work. . . . I see life's happenings, as well as art, through the wisdom of the Bible.

—Marc Chagall, Jewish artist (famous stained-glass window at Hadassah Hospital shown here)

I made my stage debut in second grade . . . as Queen Esther. . . . I wore one of my mother's striped sheets tied around me as a toga, and a birthday crown. . . . I am convinced that I have a life in the theater because of Queen Esther.

—Wendy Wasserstein, award-winning playwright

Torah and the "People of the Book"

We turn to the Torah for guidance, both as a nation and as individuals. Its stories, laws, and values are the building blocks for Jewish life, so it is not surprising that *Am Yisrael*, the Jewish people, are called the "people of the book." But it is the way Jews personally identify with the text that makes it so meaningful. Whether it is a message of hope, a significant ritual, or the story of a character's struggle, each of us can find something in the words of the Torah to relate to. As a sage advised, "Turn it [the Torah] over and over, for everything is in it." (*Pirkei Avot*, chapter 5)

Each of the people pictured here has been inspired by our sacred books. Can you think of a way in which a story in the Bible has inspired you?

I like Miriam a lot. I think she is the most important female prophet. She's really smart and cares about people.

—Samara; Glen Ridge, New Jersey

I would like to meet Isaac; he was so special because he was saved from being sacrificed.

—Saadya; Silver Spring, Maryland

The more deeply immersed I became in the thinking of the Prophets, the more powerfully it became clear to me . . . there is no limit to the concern one must feel for the suffering of human beings.

—Abraham Joshua Heschel, American rabbi and Jewish philosopher (shown here marching for civil rights with Martin Luther King Jr.)

I can't say that I understood the Psalms completely, but I sensed their spirit and felt both the joy and the suffering of King David, their author. His words lifted me.

—Natan Sharansky, former Soviet refusenik, Israeli politician (on finding hope while in prison in the former Soviet Union)

What Is Torah?

The great Jewish sage Hillel once received a challenging request. A man promised to convert to Judaism if Hillel could teach him the whole Torah as he stood on one foot. To his surprise, Hillel did as he asked, saying, "That which is hateful to you, do not do to your neighbor. That is the whole Torah; the rest is commentary. Go and study it." (Talmud, *Shabbat*, 31a)

Why do you think Hillel said that this one lesson represented the whole Torah?

Our Most Sacred Book

The Torah contains the first five books of the Bible. Written in ancient Hebrew, the holy language of Am Yisrael, the Torah is the source of many Jewish symbols and rituals, ethical teachings and laws, Jewish holidays, *mitzvot*, prayers and stories. It contains the earliest history of the Jewish people. Its lessons are relevant for all of us, and we turn to it again and again, finding new messages that shape our lives. We sometimes use the word *Torah* more broadly, to refer to all our sacred texts and all Jewish knowledge.

Words to Know: Tanakh

Did you know that the Jewish Bible is also called the **Tanakh**? The word *Tanakh* is a Hebrew acronym for the three parts of the Bible: **T**orah (also called the Five Books of Moses), **N**evi'im (Prophets), and **K**'tuvim (Writings). Nevi'im includes stories from the times of the Jewish prophets and kings in the Land of Israel. K'tuvim includes poems, proverbs, and accounts from later in our history, such as the Book of Esther, the Purim story.

תַּנַ"ךְ

תּוֹרָה

נְבִיאִים

כְּתוּבִים

6

Name That Book

How much do you already know about the Tanakh? Use the clues, available letters, and word bank to complete the names of some books of the Tanakh.

A collection of Hebrew poems, said to have been written by King David

◯ S __ __ __ S

Where it all began; the first stories of our ancestors

__ ◯ E __ __ S

A Jewish prophet who warned of the destruction of the First Temple

__ __ E ◯ __ M __ __ __ __

A famous Jewish convert who left her home to live in Israel

◯ __ T __

A book about Jewish royals __ __ N __ ◯

The famous story of how Am Yisrael was freed from slavery __ X ◯ __ __ __

Unscramble the circled letters to name one more book of the Tanakh: __ __ __ V __ __ B __

Based on its name, what do you think is in this book, and why is it part of the Bible? _____

_____

Do you know the names of any other books of the Prophets or Writings? _____

Word Bank:

Torah (Five Books of Moses)
Genesis
Exodus
Leviticus
Numbers
Deuteronomy

Nevi'im (Prophets), includes...
Joshua
Judges
Kings 1 & 2
Jeremiah
Jonah (and more)

K'tuvim (Writings) includes...
Psalms
Proverbs
Ruth
Esther
Ezra (and more)

Getting the Message Across: Written and Oral Torah

Television, the Internet, newspapers, books, videos . . . there are so many ways in which we receive information every day. This is true for how we get the messages of the Torah, too. For thousands of years, we have had both a Written Torah and an Oral Torah. The Written Torah includes the sacred texts of the Tanakh, carefully written down so the text was not changed over time. The Oral Torah, on the other hand, was originally made up of lively discussions about the Bible passed down from teachers to students for generations.

Eventually, the Oral Torah was also written down, and evolved into the *Talmud*. When we write new books based on the wisdom of the Tanakh, we add our own voices to thousands of years of commentary. This means that our understanding of the Torah is always growing, as each generation interprets its lessons for its own times.

Talk about It

David Ben-Gurion, the first prime minister of Israel, said, "We have guarded the Book for thousands of years and it has guarded us." What do you think he meant?

CHAPTER 2

TORAH: AT THE HEART OF JEWISH LIFE

"When God began to create heaven and earth . . . God said, 'Let there be light'; and there was light. God saw that the light was good, and God separated the light from the darkness. God called the light Day and the darkness Night. And there was evening and there was morning, a first day." (Genesis 1:1-4)

Have you ever used a sketch or diagram to plan out a painting or other project? Just as an architect uses a blueprint, a detailed plan, as a reference for a new building, Jewish tradition tells us that the Torah was God's plan for the world. How can we continue God's work and build a world based on the Torah?

Blueprint for Our Lives

The Torah was not only a blueprint for creating the world, but it is also a plan for leading a Jewish life. We look to the Torah to learn how to lead a better life and improve the world. The Torah gives us the language of the Jewish people, Hebrew, the basis of Jewish law, core Jewish values, 613 mitzvot, and an account of the early history that shaped Am Yisrael.

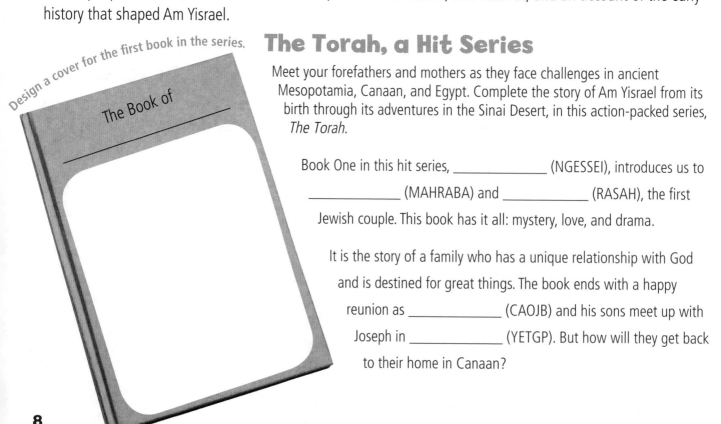

Design a cover for the first book in the series.

The Book of _____

_____

The Torah, a Hit Series

Meet your forefathers and mothers as they face challenges in ancient Mesopotamia, Canaan, and Egypt. Complete the story of Am Yisrael from its birth through its adventures in the Sinai Desert, in this action-packed series, *The Torah*.

Book One in this hit series, _____ (NGESSEI), introduces us to _____ (MAHRABA) and _____ (RASAH), the first Jewish couple. This book has it all: mystery, love, and drama.

It is the story of a family who has a unique relationship with God and is destined for great things. The book ends with a happy reunion as _____ (CAOJB) and his sons meet up with Joseph in _____ (YETGP). But how will they get back to their home in Canaan?

The second book in the series, _____ (XESDOU), opens in Egypt, where trouble is brewing for Am Yisrael. Jacob's descendants have multiplied, and _____(OHPARHA) feels threatened. It will take a palace insider, _____ (SMSEO), to save the Jewish nation. Great miracles, such as the _____ (ARGPITN) of the sea, help the Israelites escape. Book highlights include receiving the _____ _____ (NET CMMAODNMNETS) and building the Mishkan (the Tabernacle). We leave _____ _____ (MA ESIAYRL) in the desert, looking forward to returning to Canaan.

A talking _____ (EKDONY), an earthquake, battles with kings . . . what's next for Am Yisrael? The three other books in the series, Leviticus, _____ (BMEUNRS), and Deuteronomy, cover the nation's adventures in the Sinai _____ (EEDRST). From the nourishing _____ ANAMN that appears with the morning dew, to the story of the _____ (PSEIS) who gave the Land of _____ (LIESRA) a bad review, life in the desert is something to read about. We leave the Jewish nation preparing to enter Canaan, the future Land of Israel.

Write your own blurb and review of the second book in the series.

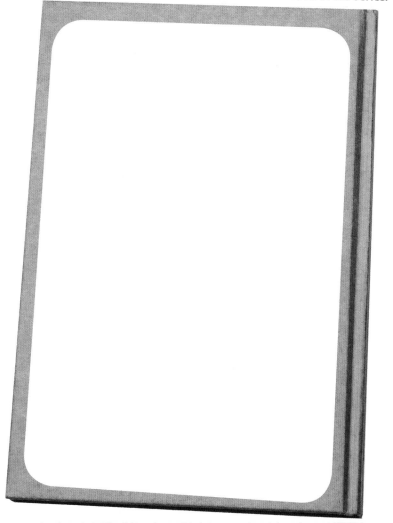

Moses, by Gustave Doré

How We Received the Torah

The Torah is close to our heart, and its text has been carefully passed down from one generation to the next. How did we get this text, which is so central to us? The Bible describes an awe-inspiring scene at Mount Sinai when God gave the Torah to Am Yisrael. This moment has also been immortalized in songs, books, movies, and more. It is this event that symbolizes the importance of the Torah as a connection to God; as a renewal of the *Brit*, the Covenant made between God and Abraham; and as the source for Jewish tradition to this day.

What actually happened at Mount Sinai? That depends on whom you ask. Different Jewish groups have varied beliefs about when and how the Torah was written. But whether you believe it was dictated by God to Moses, or inspired by God, or written by different people over time, we all share the belief that the Torah tells the story of Am Yisrael and is the source of our Jewish values, stories, and traditions.

A Text Etched in Stone: The Ten Commandments

In the Torah, we read that the Ten Commandments were carved onto two stone tablets and carried by Moses down Mount Sinai. They were kept in the Holy Ark, which was carried through the desert and into Israel, and later housed in the Temple in Jerusalem. These tablets were a physical symbol of the Brit made between God and the Jewish people at Mount Sinai. Even today, the image of the tablets signifies a commitment to the ideals of the Torah. Can you think of a place where you have seen the tablets used as a symbol? Why do you think it was there?

1. I am Adonai your God who brought you out of the land of Egypt.

2. You shall have no other gods besides Me. You shall not make idols for yourself.

3. Do not swear falsely using the name of God.

4. Remember Shabbat and keep it holy. Six days you will work, but on the seventh day you will rest.

5. Honor your father and mother.

6. Do not murder.

7. Do not be unfaithful to your wife or husband.

8. Do not steal.

9. Do not falsely accuse your neighbor.

10. Do not desire things that belong to your neighbor.

You Be the Judge

Ever since the Jewish people received the Ten Commandments, they have used them to make the world a more just place. It is not always easy to apply them, though. Consider the situations below.

Case A: A college student wants to help the homeless. He doesn't have much to give, so he goes online and breaks into a bank's accounts, then transfers the money to the charity.
What commandment did he break? _____
What should he do instead? _____

Case B: An artist makes a sculpture of God talking to Abraham, puts it in a synagogue's sanctuary, and leads the congregation in praying to it. What commandment did she break? _____
What should she do instead? _____

Case C: Soldiers are ordered to kill people who disagree with the views of the dictator.
What commandment are they breaking? _____
What should they do instead? _____

Case D: A teenager sneaks out of her house to go to a party, instead of asking her parents for permission to go.
What commandment did she break? _____
What should she do instead? _____

Can you name some other examples where the Ten Commandments are relevant in today's world?

_____

_____

What would the world be like if everyone upheld the Ten Commandments?

_____

_____

613 Mitzvot

Did you know there are actually 613 commandments, or *mitzvot*, found in the Torah? These include laws for observing holidays, rules governing business practices, values that guide how we treat one another, requirements to be kind to animals and to the earth, and much more. How many mitzvot can you list?

_____

_____

_____

_____

_____

_____

_____

Building Blocks of Jewish Identity

We learn stories and mitzvot from the Torah, and so much more. Discover how much of our Jewish identity comes from the Torah. Enter the specific building blocks of the Torah into the appropriate buildings. Some might belong in more than one building. Then choose one from each category and explain how it is a part of your Jewish life.

The Azrieli Center, Tel Aviv, Israel

Holidays

Bible Stories

Ethical Mitzvot

Ritual Mitzvot

Building Blocks: Rosh Hashanah, visiting the sick, sounding the shofar, eating matzah, Passover, receiving the Torah, Shavuot, tzedakah, honoring your parents, Sukkot, fasting on Yom Kippur, celebrating Shabbat, Abraham and Sarah move to Canaan, welcoming guests, Joseph in Egypt, sh'lom bayit, Creation, Yom Kippur, studying Torah

From Moses to Akiva: Passing It On

A Jewish legend tells how Moses, atop Mount Sinai, found God drawing crowns on some of the letters in the Torah. Moses asked what they were for and learned that in the future, a great sage, Rabbi Akiva, would study these letters and gain new insights into Jewish law. Curious, Moses asked to see more and was transported to Rabbi Akiva's classroom.

To his amazement, he could not understand the rabbi's lesson at all. Although the source of the lesson was the Torah that God gave to Moses at Mount Sinai, Rabbi Akiva was interpreting

Share What You Learn

Passing on the Torah is part of keeping the covenant between Am Yisrael and God. The Jewish people's identity is strengthened when we learn lessons from the Torah's stories and commandments, and when we share those lessons with others. Match the Torah topics below to the lessons we can all learn from that topic. Some topics might have more than one lesson, and some lessons might fit multiple topics.

Torah Topics	Lessons Learned
a. Abraham asks God to spare the people of Sodom and Gomorrah.	Thanking God
b. Miriam leads the Israelite women in song and dance after the Exodus.	Remembering our past
c. The Israelites all contribute to the building of the Tabernacle.	Compassion
	Being our best selves
d. In the desert, Moses chooses worthy judges to settle disputes between Israelites.	Paying attention to our actions
	Welcoming guests
e. The Torah commands us to blow the shofar on Rosh Hashanah.	Strengthening our community
	Working together
f. We build a sukkah on Sukkot to recall the huts in which our ancestors lived in the desert.	Hopefulness
	Judging fairly

What three Torah stories, rituals, or mitzvot would you share with someone studying the Torah for the first time? Why?

1. _____

2. _____

3. _____

it in a new way that even Moses couldn't comprehend. Then Moses understood what God was showing him—that Torah would live on because generations of Jews would continue to study it, finding new meanings in it for their own times.

What do you think the religious school of the future will look like? How will its students study the Torah?

The Sefer Torah

A long ivory-colored scroll with columns of handwritten black letters in an ancient language and spaces scattered in the middle of the text—what is this mysterious-looking object? The Torah scroll, the *sefer Torah*, may look like an artifact from the past, but in fact it is used constantly in Jewish life today. We read aloud its words, which have kept the Hebrew language alive since ancient times, and we listen to its messages, which are relevant for every moment of our day. This is no dusty artifact stored away in a museum.

Did you know that it is a mitzvah to write your own Torah scroll? Or that we kiss the Torah as it is paraded around the synagogue after a reading? What does this tell you about the role that Torah plays in our lives?

Making a Torah Scroll

A new Torah scroll is made in almost the same way as scrolls have been made for centuries. The scribe who writes a Torah is called a *sofer*, "one who counts," because every letter is important and must be accounted for. The text must be perfectly copied for a Torah to be acceptable, or "kosher." It can take as long as a year to make a Torah scroll. Identify each part of the process by matching the captions to the pictures.

a. Preparing the *k'laf* (parchment), special ink, and feather quill for writing the letters

b. Writing the Hebrew text onto each piece of parchment

c. Sewing the sheets of parchment together

d. Attaching the two ends of the scroll to the wooden rollers

e. Rolling up the scroll

Torah Rules

There are many unique laws for making a Torah scroll. Each law is designed to protect the holiness of the scroll. Here are some of them:

1. The scribe begins each day's work with a special prayer emphasizing the holiness of the task.

2. The text of a Torah scroll must be written by hand.

3. The letters must be written in permanent black ink.

4. The parchment must be made from the skin of a kosher animal.

5. The scribe cannot write the text from memory but must copy it from a correct text.

6. Each sheet of parchment must be checked by other Torah experts before it is used.

7. If the scribe makes a mistake while writing the name of God, it cannot be erased; the sheet must be buried and a new one begun.

8. Every letter and word must be perfectly spaced, and every letter must be clearly written.

Choose two rules and write a possible reason for each rule on a separate paper. How do you think these rules add to the sacredness of the Torah scroll?

Talk about It

Tell a favorite story from the Torah in your own words. Why is this story important or meaningful to you? What can we learn from it?

Words to Know: Chumash

When the Torah is printed in book form, it is also called the *chumash*. The name *chumash* comes from the Hebrew word *chameish* (five), a reminder that the chumash consists of the Five Books of Moses. Like the five fingers on a hand that can be used individually but are stronger as a unit, the five books that make up the chumash are each important but together provide the very foundation of our Jewish identity.

A Closer Look

In the 1940s and 1950s, an amazing discovery was made in caves near the Dead Sea, which is today part of modern Israel. Ancient scrolls of the Bible were uncovered, dating back to the time of the Second Temple. One of the few complete scrolls found was the Book of Isaiah, one of the prophets. Amazingly, the text is almost the same as it is in the Tanakh we use today.

CHAPTER 3

TANAKH: PROPHETS, JUDGES, AND KINGS

"...Prepare to cross the Jordan, together with all the people, into the land that I am giving to the Israelites. Every spot on which your foot treads I give to you, as I promised Moses." (Joshua 1:2-3)

When young men and women complete their basic training in the Israeli army today, one of the items they receive is a Tanakh, a Bible. Why do you think this book is given to them? Can you think of any life lessons that can be learned from its stories and personalities? Why is the Tanakh a good gift for someone starting a new phase in life?

The Story Continues

Wise judges, kings and queens, high priests, and outspoken prophets—we meet them all in the books of the Prophets and Writings. Here is where the story of Am Yisrael continues. The Prophets section of the Tanakh opens with Joshua conquering and settling Canaan, and continues with the adventures of Am Yisrael's first leaders in their own land.

The Jewish people had to learn how to run a country while remembering their Brit with God. They needed both political and spiritual leadership. Judges were appointed to govern the people, resolve disputes, and serve as military leaders. Prophets, *nevi'im* in Hebrew, kept the Jewish nation and its leaders on the right track by delivering messages from God and giving moral advice.

What qualities do you think it takes to lead Am Yisrael? List three of them here:

_____

_____

_____

Deborah, by Gustave Doré

Leading Am Yisrael

Do you know the difference between a prophet, judge, and king? Read the following words from the Prophets section of the Tanakh and identify a specific job or accomplishment of each of these leaders.

Name	Quote	Job or accomplishment
The first judge, Joshua	"…Get provisions ready, for in three days' time you are to cross the Jordan, in order to enter and possess the land that Adonai your God is giving you as a possession." (Joshua 1:11)	
King David	"Adonai has broken through my enemies before me as water breaks through [a dam]." (2 Samuel 5:20)	
King Solomon	"…I have built the House for the name of Adonai, the God of Israel, and I have set a place there for the Ark…." (1 Kings 8:20-21)	
The prophet Elijah	"How long will you keep hopping between two opinions? If Adonai is God, follow Him; and if Baal, follow him!" (1 Kings 18:21)	
The prophet Jeremiah	"…Mend your ways and your actions… conduct justice between one person and another…" (Jeremiah 7:5)	

What similarities or differences do you see in the kinds of leadership a prophet, judge, or king offered the Jewish nation?

"Who Am I?" Tic-Tac-Toe

How many leaders of Am Yisrael can you identify? Solve the clues on the game board, and see how quickly you can fill in three in a row. Or play against a friend, writing your initials in the box for each clue you solve.

Word Bank:
Deborah, Eli, Solomon, Esther, Ezra, Daniel, Joshua, Jeremiah, Elijah

The only female judge, I was famous for my wisdom and led the nation in battle. **BDOHARE**	I was the leader who led the Israelites into Israel and saw the walls of Jericho tumbling down. **SOJHAU**	I was the high priest who trained Samuel to be a leader from the time he was a young boy. **LEI**
I was the prophet in Israel who warned the Jewish nation about the destruction of the First Temple and the exile to Babylonia. **IEAEJHMR**	I was a scribe who led Jews from exile in Babylonia back to Israel and taught the Torah to the community in Jerusalem. **ZARE**	As queen, I was able to influence the king of Persia to change his mind about a terrible decree for the Jewish people. **TESHER**
An early exile to Babylonia, I was a prophet who survived a night in a den with lions. **AILEDN**	As the third king of Israel, I brought peace and wealth to the land and was able to build the first Temple. **MOSLOON**	In my role as prophet of Israel, I proved that many false prophets were lying to the people. **JLEIHA**

Writings: Wisdom for the Ages

The Bible not only teaches the history of the Jewish people but also offers all kinds of wise advice. In Writings, or *K'tuvim*, the third section of Tanakh, you will find a whole book of sayings, called Proverbs. Writings also includes books of poetry and additional historical works. The words of Tanakh have even made their way into popular culture. How many of the following sayings from the Tanakh are familiar to you? *"The writing is on the wall." "To everything there is a season." "A leopard cannot change its spots."*

Scroll Sense

You may be familiar with the **megillah**, or scroll, that we read on Purim, but did you know that Writings has five **megillot**, or scrolls—Song of Songs, Ruth, Lamentations, Ecclesiastes, and Esther—which are each read on different holidays? The Scroll of Esther almost didn't make it into the Tanakh. Some of the sages argued that it couldn't be considered sacred since it didn't mention God at all. Based on what you know about the story of Esther, why do you think it was included?

Your Turn

Turn the biblical story of Ruth or Esther into a TV miniseries.

1. Read a few chapters from or a retelling of the Book of Ruth or the Book of Esther.

2. Make an outline of the story, listing the episodes you would produce for the series.

3. Create a storyboard for your favorite episode, a series of drawings showing all the action in that part of the story.

Proverbs Advice Maven

Use Proverbs to be an advice maven, or expert. Write answers to the following letters using the wisdom found in the Book of Proverbs. Be sure to mention which proverbs guided you.

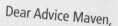

Proverbs

➤ Do not desert your friend.

➤ Speak up, judge fairly, champion the poor and the needy.

➤ Listen to advice and accept discipline in order that you may be wise in the end.

➤ Wisdom is more precious than rubies.

➤ A gentle response lightens anger; a harsh word causes it.

➤ Listen to the discipline of your father, and do not turn away from the teaching of your mother.

➤ A righteous person is concerned with the poor.

➤ Do not quarrel with a man for no reason, when he has done no harm to you.

➤ If you are lazy, go to the ant, study its ways and learn.

➤ A trustworthy person keeps a confidence.

Dear Advice Maven,

My best friend and I know all of each other's secrets. But recently, at a friend's sleep-over party, I overheard her telling a couple of other friends some of my secrets! So I said things to her that weren't so nice. Now she's mad at me. What should I do? I don't want to lose her as a friend.

Losing Sleep

Dear Losing Sleep, _____

_____

_____

Dear Advice Maven,

My parents limit how much television I watch to one show a day, telling me it's for my own good. I really feel left out at school when my friends talk about all these shows I miss, but my parents won't budge. I figured out how to watch them on my computer, while my parents think I'm doing homework. Since I still get all my homework done, is this OK?

Tired of the Rules

Dear Tired of the Rules, _____

_____

_____

Dear Advice Maven,

I live in a big city. Sometimes when I go to the park, I see homeless people. It makes me so sad to see people sleeping in cardboard boxes. I really want to help them. My friend says that a lot of them use the money people give them to buy alcohol or drugs, and that it would be better if I contributed to a charity. What is the best way to help?

Looking to Help

Dear Looking to Help, _____

_____

_____

Dear Advice Maven,

I am part of an after-school science club. A few of us want to enter a competition, which would mean spending extra time researching our project on weekends. I don't want to stop hanging out with my friends, but I am also excited about the competition. How do I decide?

Missing Out

Dear Missing Out, _____

_____

_____

Voices from the Past

From a young musician defeating a giant, to a queen risking her life to save the Jewish people, the heroes and heroines of the Tanakh inspire us to be the best versions of ourselves. We study the stories and texts of the Bible closely, paying attention to the actions and words of its characters. We learn from their example, by the ways they navigated the world and lived according to Jewish values despite the challenges they encountered. Complete this crossword puzzle by identifying the values we learn from these biblical voices.

David, **Andrea del Castagno, 15th century**

Word Bank:
Courage
Hospitality
Kindness
Loyalty
Remembrance
Wisdom

Across:

4. Moses urged _____ when he told the Israelites, *"Remember this day, on which you went free from Egypt, the house of bondage."* (Exodus 13:3)

5. King Solomon was known for _____, and prayed to God, *"Give Your servant an understanding mind to judge Your people, to distinguish between good and bad."* (1 Kings 3:9)

6. Ruth showed _____ when she said to her mother-in-law, *"Wherever you go, I will go . . . your people shall be my people, and your God shall be my God."* (Ruth 1:16)

Down:

1. Abraham offered _____ when he said to the visiting angels, *"Rest under the tree. I will get a morsel of bread for you to refresh yourselves. Then you can continue on your way."* (Genesis 18:4-5)

2. Queen Esther demonstrated _____ when she said, *"I shall go to the king, though it is contrary to the law; and if I am to perish, I shall perish!"* (Esther 4:16)

3. Rebecca offered _____ when she told Abraham's servant, *"Let me draw water for your camels, so they can drink their fill."* (Genesis 24:19)

Choose two of the quotes and explain what the characters were thinking, and what we learn from this.

_____

_____

You Take the Good, You Take the Bad

The Tanakh also shows us the flaws of Jewish heroes. We learn not only from their wisdom, but also from their mistakes and poor choices. The story of Joseph's life shows how one crime affected a famous biblical family. Be a biblical detective and figure out what happened.

The Case of the Many-Colored Coat

Joseph's brothers bring their father, Jacob, the blood-stained coat of many colors that had belonged to Joseph. Jacob assumes that Joseph was killed by a wild animal and mourns for him. But his body has not been found. What happened to Joseph?

Missing Person Report

Name: Joseph, son of Jacob and Rachel

M/F: male   *Age:* 17   *Address:* Canaan

Description: Wears a many-colored coat given to him by his father; known to have grand dreams about his whole family bowing down to him

Last seen: Wandering the fields in Canaan, looking for his brothers who were tending to their father's flocks

Talk about It

Why do you think the Tanakh records both the good and the bad actions of Jewish heroes?

Evidence

Found at the scene: Leftovers of a meal, piece of silver, deep pit in the desert, slaughtered goat, camel tracks

Caught on tape: "Here comes the dreamer! Come now *(sounds of a struggle)*. . . .We can say that a wild beast ate him. Then let's see what will become of his dreams!" . . . "Don't kill him. . . . Throw him into this pit in the desert. . . ." *(Camel sounds, from a traveling caravan.)* "Let's sell him to the Ishmaelites. . . . " (from Genesis 37:1-36)

Travel itinerary of Ishmaelite traders: From Canaan to Egypt, carrying gum, balsam, resin, and slaves

What happened? How do you know?

_____

What flaws do Joseph and his brothers demonstrate?

_____

Years later, Joseph has become a powerful Egyptian official, and he forgives his brothers. Find out what happens by reading Genesis 45:1-8. What lessons can we learn from the story of Joseph?

_____

_____

CHAPTER 4

READING SACRED TEXTS:
A YEAR OF JEWISH BOOKS

"This is the Torah that Moses placed before the children of Israel, at the word of Adonai, by the hand of Moses." (Deuteronomy 4:44, Numbers 9:23. Recited as the Torah is lifted before the congregation.)

Think about your favorite books. Where do you keep them and how do you use them? Jewish sacred books are meant to be used, not left to gather dust on a high shelf. Generations of Jews have used them every day for studying, praying, teaching, and more. Can you think of some times when Jewish books are used during the year?

Torah for the Jewish Community

The sages knew that to keep the Torah alive, it needed to be part of daily Jewish life, so they scheduled Torah readings into the Jewish calendar. Back in biblical days, Am Yisrael used to travel to Jerusalem on Sukkot every seven years to hear the Torah read aloud. Later, it became the custom to read parts of the Torah each week when people gathered together on Shabbat and on market days. Why do you think the Torah scroll is read only when a **minyan**, a gathering of at least ten Jewish adults, is present?

In some congregations, the entire Torah scroll is unrolled during Simḥat Torah celebrations.

An Everlasting Torah Loop

The sages wanted the Jewish community to become very familiar with the stories and lessons in the Five Books of Moses. So they set up a Torah reading schedule that is an everlasting loop—the Five Books are divided into portions, and each week we read the next portion, or ***parashah***, until the whole Torah is read. We finish reading the Torah scroll on the holiday of Simḥat Torah, when we read the last parashah and rejoice with the Torah, dancing and singing over it. But there is little time to rest—immediately we read from the very beginning of the Torah, and the cycle begins again. Why do you think we begin again so quickly?

The cycle of Torah reading dates back to ancient times. Many traditional communities follow the custom of Babylonian Jews from Talmudic times, which is to complete the whole Torah every year. Other congregations choose to follow a three-year cycle, as Jews in ancient Israel did. Find out which custom your synagogue follows.

Your Turn

Write a letter or blog entry that describes a Shabbat Torah service or a Simḥat Torah celebration in your synagogue. Be sure to note anything that you found interesting or surprising, as well as any questions you might have.

How Reading the Torah Unites Am Yisrael

In 1981, a small group of Americans traveled to a remote Jewish village in Ethiopia to explore how they could help the community fight famine, disease, and persecution. One traveler recalls what it took for the villagers and her group to connect:

The village was very poor and very much a culture shock. . . . Everyone was barefoot. . . . The houses were mud huts. And when we asked to be taken to the synagogue, it was a hut; only a stone hut, empty inside. When we asked to see their Torah, they went and got it for us, and it wasn't a scroll, it was a book. And it wasn't written in Hebrew, it was written in Ge'ez [ancient Ethiopian language]. What I was feeling then was . . . we were so different. . . . How were we possibly going to connect, make any friendships? And then somebody in the group asked what parashah they were reading that week, and it turned out that they were reading parashat Noah, and back home in America we were reading parashat Noah, and that was just an amazing, transcending moment. . . . The fact that we were all on the same page. . . . All of a sudden all of the differences just stopped having any meaning and we were just a bunch of Jews together in a Jewish community.

—Barbara Ribakove Gordon, founder and executive director of the North American Conference on Ethiopian Jewry

An Ethiopian Jewish priest holds the *Orit*, the Ethiopian Torah, 1984.

Judging the Torah by Its Cover

Although we are taught not to judge a book by its cover, in the case of the Torah scroll, its appearance tells us a lot about what's inside. Think about the Torah scrolls that you have seen. How are they dressed? Just as clothing can express an identity, the way a Torah is decorated says something about what it holds inside.

Yad (Torah pointer)

_____

What the Torah Wears

The beautiful objects that adorn the Torah scroll each have a purpose. Take a look at these Torahs, which are dressed according to Ashkenazi (European) custom. How do you think each of the items is used? Write your answers on the lines.

Binder

_____

Crown

_____

Rimmonim (finials)

_____

Atzei ḥayyim
(rollers, Hebrew for "trees of life")

_____

Mantle (cover)

_____

Torah shield

_____

A silver Torah case, called a *tik*, is typically used by Jewish communities from Middle Eastern countries.

Words to Know:
Aliyah

During the Torah reading, congregants may be called up to the Torah to recite blessings before and after each section. This honor is called an *aliyah*, which means "going up." Why do you think this tradition is associated with the idea of going up?

A Day in the Life of a Torah Scroll

The Torah is read regularly during the week and on holidays. The busiest day for a Torah scroll is Shabbat. The scroll is usually kept in the Holy Ark in the synagogue, but on Saturday morning it is taken out for the Shabbat Torah reading. Every part of the ceremony shows how much the Jewish community values the Torah. Use the word bank to complete the sentences below.

Getting Out: On Shabbat morning, I am dressed up in my finest embroidered _____, with shiny pomegranate-shaped _____ on my *atzei ḥayyim* (rollers). I hear singing, and suddenly the doors of the _____ swing open! I am carried across the _____ while the congregation watches.

Opening Up: My adornments are set aside, and I am gently placed down on the _____. My _____ are rolled so that the scroll is open to today's Torah portion. A congregant comes up for the first _____, recites the blessing over the Torah, and we are off!

The Reading: The reader uses the _____ to point to the spot where the Torah reading begins. Another person follows along in a printed _____. If a mistake is made, the reader is corrected. Each week, a different _____ is read or chanted aloud.

Closing Time: The reading ends. I am lifted high for everyone to see my beautiful words and then rolled closed, tied with the _____, and covered again. I am held while I listen to the words of the *Haftarah* (the selection from Prophets) and the _____ that follow. Then everyone stands and sings joyfully as I am returned to my home in the Ark.

> **Word Bank:** Ark, bimah, reader's desk, parashah, chumash, blessings, yad, *atzei ḥayyim*, mantle, rimmonim, binder, aliyah

Meet Samara

Samara balances trumpet practice, homework, and a love of Torah. She worked hard to prepare for her bat mitzvah, and had a memorable and meaningful celebration.

Preparing for My Bat Mitzvah: About a year or so before the bat mitzvah, I started reading the parashah with a tutor once a week. I learned to read with the *trope*, the special chant. I read the Hebrew before learning the chant and practiced a *lot*.

Reading the Parashah: I helped lead part of the prayer service, starting with the Sh'ma. I chanted the whole parashah and also some of the Haftarah. I also gave the *d'var Torah*, a talk about the parashah. The hardest part was getting up in front of people and singing, but it was okay. I like the sound of the trope—it's calming—and then I focused on what I was doing.

Torah in My Life: When I was little, I went up with my parents to watch as they read the Torah. I liked to see the Torah scroll, and I used to just stare at the Torah up close. This year I volunteered to read the Haftarah on Shabbat, and even part of the parashah on Yom Kippur. I hope to continue to do this.

Biblical Links

Make time in your schedule to meet Ruth, Jonah, and Esther each year, since we also read selections from the Prophets and Writings on Shabbat and holidays. The **Haftarah**, the selection from Prophets we read after the Torah portion, is linked to themes in the weekly parashah and so reinforces its lessons. Why do we read the Haftarah? The Ḥanukkah story offers one explanation: when the Greek ruler at that time, Antiochus, banned the reading of the Torah, the Jews began to read related material from Prophets instead.

On certain Jewish holidays, we read **megillot**, scrolls from Writings that reinforce the themes of those holidays.

Holiday Connections

Can you find the connection between the holidays and their Haftarah or megillah readings? Draw lines to match each Haftarah or megillah to the holiday on which we read it. Hint: Use the highlighted words to help you find a match. How do these readings add to the meaning of the holiday?

What we read	When we read it
Jonah: In this book, we read about how Jonah was sent to tell the people of Nineveh to **repent** and was swallowed by a big fish.	**Simhat Torah**, a time of endings and beginnings, when we finish our cycle of reading the Torah and begin again
1 Kings: This book describes how King Solomon built and dedicated the First **Temple**.	**Yom Kippur**, when we repent for our mistakes and promise to become our best selves in the new year
Joshua: This book describes a time of new **beginnings** as Joshua becomes the leader of Am Yisrael after Moses's death.	**Tisha B'Av**, when we mourn the destruction of the Temple in Jerusalem
Lamentations: This megillah tells about the **destruction** of Jerusalem and exile of the Jewish nation.	**Sukkot**, the fall holiday on which Jews since ancient times have made a pilgrimage (traveled) to the Temple
Esther: In this megillah, we learn the story of how the Jewish people were **saved** from destruction in Persia.	**Shavuot**, when we celebrate receiving the Torah at Mount Sinai
Ruth: This megillah tells the story of how Ruth, great-grandmother of King David, accepted God and the **Torah**.	**Purim**, when we celebrate how our people foiled the evil plans of Haman and were saved

Megillat Esther: A Purim Turnaround

Listening to *Megillat Esther*, the Book of Esther, being read on Purim is one of the main mitzvot of the holiday, and the Jewish community actively participates by drowning out Haman's name. The Purim tale is one in which events turn around very quickly. Its characters' fortunes rise and fall, as does the fate of the Jewish people. For example, Haman is an important official in the Persian palace, but by the end of the megillah he has lost his position and his life. The Jewish people, on the other hand, are under threat of being wiped out but then rejoice when the evil decree is overturned.

What lessons do you think the megillah is teaching us? _____

_____

Can you think of a situation in which one of these lessons might help you? _____

_____

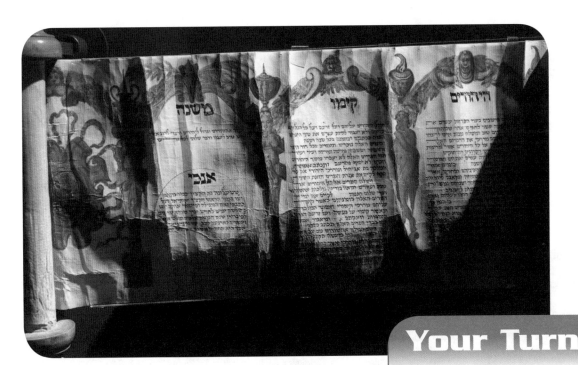

How does the Scroll of Esther, read on Purim, look different from the Torah scroll used every Shabbat?

Your Turn

Costumes and masks give us a chance to explore different sides of our identity. Make a double-sided mask for Purim or anytime that reflects two aspects of your identity. For example, if your name is David and you like Jewish music, you might illustrate your royal namesake King David on one side and your musical tastes on the other. You decide which side of the mask will face out. You can unmask your secret side by turning the mask around at any point.

Bringing the Story Home

Most of our holiday readings, whether from the Torah, Haftarah, or megillot, are held in the community, usually in the synagogue. But on Passover, we also bring the story into our homes. For this, we use another Jewish book, the haggadah. The haggadah combines biblical passages and other texts to help us accomplish the most important mitzvah of the seder, remembering the Exodus. You can still see wine stains on the pages of old handcrafted *haggadot* from centuries ago, a sign that these haggadot were well used. Every part of the haggadah is designed to make the story and the message of freedom meaningful and relevant to us. New versions of the haggadah are created each year that help us apply its lessons to our own lives and times. Why do you think we read the haggadah at home, or at the homes of family and friends?

A Picture Is Worth a Thousand Words

You might have noticed that there are no pictures in a Torah scroll, only words. It's a different case with the haggadah. Many haggadot are beautifully illustrated, some hand-painted with real gold decoration. Full-page illustrations serve to retell the Passover story, sometimes using panels almost like a comic book.

Sarajevo haggadah

Rylands haggadah

Golden haggadah

Do a creative retelling of the Exodus story. Draw your favorite scenes from the Exodus in comic-strip form. Refer to the haggadah or to your favorite Bible story from the Book of Exodus to find the parts of the story that most appeal to you.

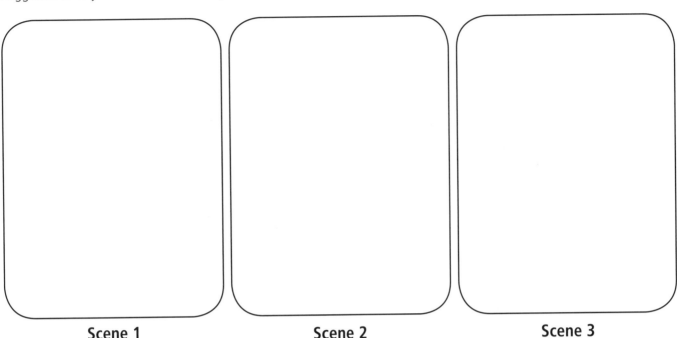

Scene 1   **Scene 2**   **Scene 3**

A Year Full of Jewish Books

There are so many opportunities throughout the year to read our sacred Jewish texts, from the Torah and Haftarah portions we read each week on Shabbat, to the Book of Jonah on Yom Kippur, Megillat Esther on Purim, the haggadah on Passover, the Book of Ruth on Shavuot, and more. Without duplicating, circle the names of all the books from the Tanakh that you can find in chapters 1 through 4. How many did you circle? _____ How could you find out the names of all of the books in the Tanakh?

In the chapters that follow, we will learn about a different kind of Jewish text—the books of laws, stories, legends, and wisdom that our ancestors have written through the ages in an attempt to more fully understand the Tanakh—and we will explore what makes a text sacred.

Talk about It

Why do you think we read the Torah and other Jewish texts consistently through the year?

How does reading Jewish sacred texts together in the community bring the Jewish people together? How does reading them at home strengthen the Jewish community, too?

29

CHAPTER 5

THE TALMUD: TEXTS OF THE SAGES

"Ben Bag Bag said: Turn it (Torah) and turn it again, for everything is in it. Contemplate it, grow old and gray in it, and do not move from it, for you can have no better guide in life than it." (Pirkei Avot 5:26)

Have you ever watched old family videos from long ago? You might laugh at the old-fashioned hairstyles, but these videos offer a fascinating peek into another time. Similarly, our sacred Jewish books give us glimpses into the lives of Jews in the past. We see this throughout the Tanakh and in the conversations, advice, stories, and teachings of our sages.

Filling in the Details

The crowning accomplishment of the Jewish sages, the **Talmud,** is a collection of writings that forms the basis of Jewish law and tradition. The Talmud goes hand-in-hand with the Tanakh, providing explanations when the Tanakh doesn't give enough detail. For example, in the Torah, Am Yisrael is given the mitzvah of keeping Shabbat: "Remember Shabbat and keep it holy. Six days you will work, but on the seventh day you will rest." (Exodus 20:8-10) But how should we celebrate it? What should the day of rest look like? This is where the Talmud comes in, providing specific laws, such as making Kiddush, lighting Shabbat candles, and not doing work.

Saving the Torah

In the year 68 CE, Jerusalem was under siege by the Romans. While Jews argued about whether or not to surrender, the sage Rabbi Yoḥanan ben Zakkai knew that real survival for the Jewish nation depended on the Torah. So he carried out a secret plan. He had his students smuggle him out of Jerusalem in a wooden coffin. Then he made his way to the Roman camp, where he told the Roman general that he would soon become emperor. When this prediction came true, the new emperor rewarded the rabbi by offering to grant him a request.

"Give me Yavneh and its scholars!" Rabbi Yoḥanan ben Zakkai asked. With this brief but strategic request, he ensured that the Torah would survive even when everything was about to change for the Jewish people. How? He built a school in the town of Yavneh. When the Temple and Jerusalem were destroyed, the sages were able to continue Torah study in Yavneh and create a new approach to Jewish life that wasn't centered on the Temple.

Meet the Sages

As Torah study grew in importance and became the focus of Judaism, its experts, the sages, led the way. They studied the Torah, interpreting its words and applying them to daily Jewish life. They started Jewish schools of learning; studied and debated Jewish law; and offered new laws, stories, legends, and advice to future generations. Join in the discussion by responding to their comments.

Statue of ancient Roman general, about 100 CE

Hillel

"If I am not for myself, who will be for me? But if I am only for myself, who am I? If not now, when?"
(Pirkei Avot 1:14)

Tell Hillel what his famous quote means to you, or describe a situation in which it applies to your life.

_____

_____

_____

_____

"Make your Torah study a fixed routine. Say little, do much. Greet everyone with a cheerful countenance."
(Pirkei Avot 1:15)

Shammai

Describe to Shammai how following his advice would change your day.

_____

_____

_____

_____

Tarfon

Rabbi Tarfon would bend down and let his mother step on him when she wanted to climb into her bed.
(Talmud, Kiddushin 31b)

Why do you think he did this? What can we learn about how to practice a mitzvah from this tale?

_____

_____

_____

Meir & Beruryah

There were once some robbers who caused Rabbi Meir a great deal of trouble. Rabbi Meir prayed that they would die. His wife, Beruryah, reminded him that in the Book of Psalms it is written, "Let sins cease." Sins, not sinners. She urged him instead to pray that the robbers would repent, and then their sins would cease.
(based on the Talmud, Berachot 10a)

Tell Meir and Beruryah what Jewish value you learn from this story.

_____

_____

_____

Laying Down the Law

When you open a page of the Talmud, you open a window into the debates of sages from long ago, as they argued the fine points of Jewish law. This is because the Talmud is the written version of the Oral Torah, the centuries of discussion and debate between teachers and students. The Oral Torah was finally written down, around the year 200 CE, by the great sage Rabbi Judah HaNasi. Rabbi Judah feared that it would otherwise be forgotten, as Jews were increasingly scattered around the world. His work, called the *Mishnah*, was studied in great depth and was the source of even more discussion in schools in the Land of Israel and Babylonia. Ultimately, these conversations were also written down and became the Jerusalem Talmud, written in Hebrew, and the Babylonian Talmud, written in Aramaic (the main language used by Jews in Babylonia). Today, the Talmud (usually the Babylonian one) is the go-to book for exploring Jewish law. In its pages, you can hear the voices of the sages, teaching us the Oral Torah. Why do you think they wrote down not just the laws but all their discussions, too?

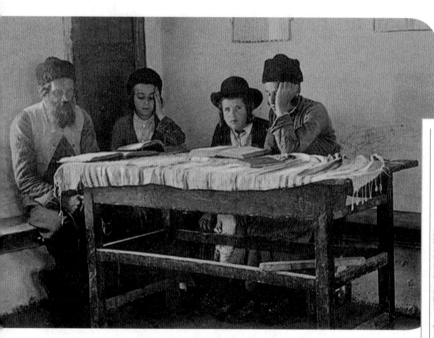

Boys studying Talmud, Palestine, 1912

A page of Talmud

Words to Know:
Mishnah, Gemara, Talmud

The names for the books of the sages, the **Mishnah** and **Talmud**, are both related to Hebrew words meaning "study" or "learning." The Mishnah was written first, followed by discussions of the Mishnah, which are called the *Gemara*. The Talmud is made up of the Mishnah, the Gemara, and several commentaries, which are discussed in Chapter 6.

Navigating the Sea of Talmud

The Talmud is compared to a deep and vast sea. In it you can find many treasures, such as the how-to's for mitzvot that are only briefly mentioned in the Torah. Unscramble the words to discover some of the topics found in the Talmud. Use the clues in the treasure chest to help.

SSGBILESN _____ to say over food

How to write a RTHAO _____ scroll

How not to waste natural ESCORRUSE _____

How to ask a EFDRIN _____ for forgiveness

When to say MHA'S _____

How to conduct a DSERE _____

How to build a KUSKAH _____

How to UTRNER _____ lost items

How to care for SAMINLA _____

Animals	Seder
Blessings	Sh'ma
Food	Shabbat
Friend	Shofar
Resources	Sukkah
Rest	Torah
Return	Tzedakah

Choose three mitzvot and explain why you think they're valuable.

_____

_____

_____

Respect for All Opinions

One interesting feature of the Talmud is that it includes lively discussions and even opposing opinions about the details of Jewish law. The Talmud tells a story about one of the most famous debates, between the students of Rabbis Hillel and Shammai. They argued for three long years over whose interpretations of the Torah should be the law. Finally, a message came from heaven that even though both were right, the law would be decided according to Hillel's students, in part because they showed respect for the followers of Shammai's explanations by studying them, too. (from Talmud, *Eruvin* 13b)

Why is respect for other opinions so important? _____

_____

Midrash: Shedding Light on the Bible

How did Abraham come to believe in one God? What was Moses's life like growing up in Pharaoh's palace? How was the spot for building the Temple chosen? The Bible leaves a lot up to our imagination. Here, too, the sages step in to help us by giving us more information about biblical people and events. We find their interpretations of the Torah's stories in the Talmud and in books of **Midrash**. The word *midrash* means "to investigate" or "search;" the sages carefully searched the words of the Bible, learning from its details. Today, people are still mining the biblical text for its lessons and creating new kinds of midrash.

Noah's Diary

You have probably heard the story of Noah and the ark many times. But the biblical account doesn't tell us everything we might want to know. For example, how did Noah and his family take care of all those animals? What was life like in the ark? The Midrash and Talmud add more to the picture. Read the items below from the midrash about Noah's time in the ark and then write a diary or blog entry from his perspective, based on these interpretations and what you know about Noah already. Include sketches, too, if you'd like.

[Noah] knew which animal was to be fed in the second hour of the day and which beast was to be fed in the third hour of the night.

(Genesis Rabbah 29:4)

One of the lions, having become enraged at Noah, attacked and injured him, so that he remained lame for the rest of his life. Noah, during the twelve months that he was in the ark, did not sleep one moment.

(Midrash Tanḥuma)

[Noah's son said:] "We had so much trouble in the ark. The animals that usually feed by day, we fed by day; and those that normally feed at night, we fed by night. But my father didn't know what food the chameleon ate. One day he was sitting and cutting up a pomegranate, when a worm dropped out of it, which [the chameleon] ate. From then on he mashed up bran for him, and when it became wormy, [the chameleon] ate it. . . ."

(Talmud, Sanhedrin 108b)

_____
_____
_____
_____
_____
_____

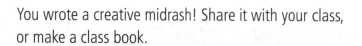

You wrote a creative midrash! Share it with your class, or make a class book.

Biblical Art Gallery

Not only have scholars created *midrashim*, but artists of all kinds have retold and interpreted biblical stories, using their imagination to depict biblical events and personalities. Since the Torah came with no pictures, these artists got creative at filling in the gaps. Their art gives us another way to look at biblical stories.

How does each piece of biblical art shown here explain or interpret the biblical story?

The Tower of Babel, Pieter Brueghel the Elder, 1563

Moses Receiving the Ten Commandments,
Marc Chagall, 1966

The Songs of Joy, James Tissot, 1902

Jonah Swallowed by the Whale, Italian mosaic, 4th century

Your Turn

Create a visual midrash. Many artists have imagined what King David looked like. Now you try: sketch a portrait of the young David based on the biblical text below and your imagination.

> "I have seen [David,] a son of Jesse . . . who is skilled in music; he is strong and a warrior . . . and handsome…." (1 Samuel 16:18)

> He took his stick, picked a few smooth stones from the stream, put them in the pocket of his shepherd's bag, and, sling in hand, he went toward the Philistine. (1 Samuel 17:40)

What information was not provided? Could you find it anywhere else? What did you have to imagine?

Talk about It

Why do you think it is important to keep studying and interpreting Jewish texts in each generation?

CHAPTER 6

THE REST IS COMMENTARY

"The Bible is a seed, God is the sun, but we are the soil. Every generation is expected to bring forth new understandings, new realizations."

(Abraham Joshua Heschel)

A boy in Australia uploads a video of his bar mitzvah speech, a teacher in California posts her students' Tanakh project on a synagogue web page, a programmer studies the Talmud on his cell phone during a lunch break. Today, as never before, the Torah is being studied, taught, and shared in many different forms around the world. How can you get involved?

Continuing the Conversation

During medieval times, Jews moved farther and farther across the world and built many new Jewish communities. They spoke different languages and developed unique customs. They also found new ways to study their sacred texts and had many questions about how the texts applied to Jewish life in their time. So more and more books of commentary, explanations of the Tanakh and Talmud, were written—and are still being created. These works continue the conversation between Jews of today and Jews of the past.

Biblical Commentary: Seventy Faces of the Torah

When two Jews are debating a point in Torah, the argument is often laid to rest when they agree to disagree, remembering these words from the Midrash, "There are seventy faces to the Torah!" What do you think this midrash means?

_____

_____

_____

Can you think of a time when you settled an argument by agreeing to disagree?

Interview with Rashi

We credit a French medieval scholar with inventing the concept of Jewish commentary. Rabbi Solomon ben Isaac (1040-1105), known by the acronym Rashi, probably never thought that his commentaries would become bestsellers for the ages. But even a thousand years after he wrote them, his insightful interpretations of the Tanakh and Talmud are talked about by students of all ages.

Sixteenth-century woodcut of Rashi

An interview with Rashi in the eleventh century might have looked something like this:

Q: How did you become such a great scholar?

A: As a young man, I studied at the great *yeshivot*, Jewish schools, in the towns of Worms and Mainz, in Germany, before returning to my hometown of Troyes in France.

Q: Where did you work?

A: I served on the Jewish rabbinical court, the *beit din*, where it was my job to help answer questions about Jewish law. I was even promoted to the head of the beit din. I also opened my own *yeshiva*, which became very popular. And I managed a vineyard.

Q: Wow, that's a lot of jobs. Why did you start writing commentary, too?

A: I saw that many Jews in my time needed help understanding the Tanakh and Talmud. So I began writing down explanations of the Bible, bringing in points from the Midrash and Talmud to help. The Talmud can be very challenging to study, so I wrote a commentary on that also. That way I could reach many more people than just the students in my yeshiva.

Q: What was your most important accomplishment?

Rashi's answer to that last question is missing. How do you think he might have responded?

_____

Now you be the interviewer. What questions do you have for Rashi?

_____

_____

Keeping Torah in the Family

Rashi passed on his love of Torah study to his children and grandchildren. In addition to his accomplished sons-in-law and grandsons, his daughters, Yocheved, Miriam, and Rachel, named after biblical heroines, were also scholars. Growing up in a household where Torah study was a focus, they had greater opportunities to study the Tanakh and Talmud than most Jewish women of the time did. They and their daughters were role models for other Jewish women, both for how they kept Jewish traditions and for teaching Torah to women in their community. Describe someone who is a Jewish role model in your community.

Meet Commentators of the Bible

Generations of rabbis and scholars have studied the Tanakh and Talmud. Their commentaries continue to help us understand and define Jewish practices today. Meet some commentators who followed in Rashi's footsteps.

Rashbam
(Rabbi Samuel ben Meir)

Lived: France; c.1085-1174

Best known for: His commentary on the Torah, explaining its plain meaning.

Torah study tip: Keep it simple.

Famous relation: He was Rashi's grandson.

Can you think of a time when you came up with a good answer by keeping it simple?

_____

_____

Ibn Ezra
(Rabbi Abraham ibn Ezra)

Lived: Spain, and traveled to England, Italy, and France;1089-1164

Best known for: His writing, from poetry, to philosophy, to biblical commentary.

Torah study tip: Pay careful attention to the grammar.

How does paying careful attention to details help you when you're reading?

_____

_____

Nachmanides
(Rabbi Moses ben Nachman, also called Ramban)

Lived: Spain and Israel; 1194-1270

Best known for: Defending Judaism in a famous debate with a Christian friar.

Torah study tip: Appreciate the hidden messages in the Torah.

How can looking for deeper meanings help you understand a story or lesson?

_____

_____

Sforno
(Rabbi Obadiah ben Jacob Sforno)

Lived: Italy; 1475-1550

Best known for: His writings on the Torah and philosophy.

Torah study tip: Use your knowledge of philosophy to help you.

How can knowledge of other subjects help when you are studying something new?

_____

_____

Questions from Many Lands

When should an astronaut celebrate Shabbat in space? Can we eat veal if the animal suffers when it is being raised? Can electricity be used on Shabbat? As time passed, and as Jews moved farther and farther across the globe, they found that they had all kinds of questions about how to live a Jewish life in new places and times. Even when they turned to the Talmud, they couldn't always find the answers they needed. Well-known rabbis such as Maimonides and Joseph Karo addressed the problem by writing user-friendly books to help Jews remember *halachah*, Jewish law.

Statue of Maimonides in Cordoba, Spain

Serving Up Jewish Law

Maimonides was a twelfth-century Torah scholar, philosopher, and physician to the sultan of Egypt. Also known as Rambam, an acronym for his full name, Rabbi Moses ben Maimon, he had a great impact in his own time and for generations of Jews, even to this day. One of his most important works was the *Mishneh Torah*, the first book that organized Jewish law by topic, making it easy for people to find answers to their questions. A popular saying states, "From Moses [of the Torah] to Moses [Maimonides], there was none like Moses." What do you think this expression means?

_____

One of the most well-known books of Jewish law is the *Shulḥan Aruch*, Hebrew for the "Set Table." Its author was Joseph Karo, a sixteenth-century rabbi from Spain and Turkey who felt that it was important to unite all Jews by giving them one set of guidelines to follow. But it didn't include the customs of Jews from Germany, France, and Poland, so a Polish rabbi, Moses Isserles, added a commentary called the *Mappah*, the "Tablecloth." Now one book could be used by Jews everywhere. Why do you think Joseph Karo gave his book the title "Set Table"? _____

Words to Know:
Halachah

The Hebrew word for Jewish law, *halachah*, is related to the word *walk*. How do you think living according to Jewish law is like walking on a path? Modern times bring new questions about halachah. For example, can you be considered part of a minyan if you join via Skype? Write down your questions relating to Jewish law in your life.

A replica of the Gutenberg press at the International Printing Museum in California

How Technology Changed Things

In medieval times, studying the Torah or the Talmud meant having a handwritten copy of the text in front of you and other handwritten books with the texts of different commentaries around you. Copying books by hand was a slow, painstaking process, which limited their availability. Then technology changed things. Johannes Gutenberg invented the printing press in the fifteenth century, allowing books to be produced much more quickly and affordably. Soon more people learned to read and were able to discuss the ideas they discovered in books. One of the first books produced on a printing press was the Bible, in 1450.

Printing became very popular in the Jewish community because Torah study was highly valued. Sacred books were printed and studied more widely than before, and shared with Jewish communities across the world. A new book called the *Mikra'ot Gedolot*, or Rabbinic Bible, made Torah study easier by including the words of multiple commentaries on the same page as the text of the Bible or Talmud.

Modern Takes

In modern times, digital technology has helped Jews study the Torah in new ways, and with those who live far away. All kinds of modern media help us interpret and share our sacred texts and our Jewish experiences, including art, music, video games, movies, television, websites, blogs, social media, and even mobile apps. We use these tools to offer modern retellings of biblical stories, or to share our opinions and feelings about Jewish subjects.

What are some examples of modern Jewish commentary that you have encountered?

_____

_____

_____

_____

_____

Your Turn

Be a commentator. Choose a piece of biblical text—either from a favorite Bible story or from this week's *parashah*, Torah portion. Write your thoughts—your commentary—about it: What do you think it means? What questions do you have about it?

Jewish Books of Note: From Sacred to Secular

The Jewish library has continued to expand. While many texts, such as the Tanakh and Talmud, are considered sacred, others are secular, such as books of Jewish fiction and biographies about Jewish leaders. All kinds of writers have made their contributions to Jewish culture, from rabbis explaining Jewish law to writers penning poems. If you're interested in Jewish folktales, humor, history, philosophy, poetry, or any other subject, there is a book out there for you. What are your favorite Jewish books?

_____

_____

In Search of the Sacred

The Torah and all of our sacred Jewish texts are called *sifrei kodesh* in Hebrew. How can a book be *kodesh*, holy? How are our Jewish sacred texts different from other books or written materials that you use? Complete the chart to see.

Talk about It

From printing to the Internet, Jews have jumped at the chance to use modern technology so that more people can read and study the Torah. What does this show about how we value Torah study?

	Jewish sacred books	Secular books
Name some examples.		
What are they about?		
When were they written?		
How do we treat them?		
What language are they in?		
When and how do we use them?		

What do you think makes Jewish sacred texts holy or special? _____

_____

CHAPTER 7

THE SIDDUR: WORDS FROM THE HEART

"I will sing and chant praises to Adonai. God, hear my voice when I call. Be gracious to me and answer me...." (from Psalm 27)

Have you ever found it hard to speak up or to ask for something? Sometimes it helps to have written notes or suggestions. The sages knew this, and so they wrote down the words to many prayers, which were later collected in the *siddur*, the Jewish prayer book. How can the words of the siddur help you express your feelings?

An Alef-Bet Prayer

A Jewish folktale tells the story of a little boy who could not read but wanted to join in *t'filah* (prayer) with the community in the synagogue. So he said the *alef bet*, *"Alef, bet, gimmel, dalet, hay...,"* asking God to take the letters and put them together to make up the words of the prayers.

Spoken with feeling, even the simple alef bet can be a prayer. The Talmud teaches us that it is a mitzvah to pray and that we should pray from the heart. But we also have many written prayers, and we have set times to say them. The sages developed prayers using the words of the Tanakh and adding subjects they felt were important, such as remembering the ancient Temple or appreciating the natural world. New prayers are still added to the siddur to this day. What subjects do you think should be included in daily prayer?

Words to Know:
Siddur, Siddurim

The first Jewish prayer books, or *siddurim*, were put together in medieval times. Since then, new prayers and special versions of the **siddur** for different communities have been created, but the basic format remains the same. There are prayer books with just the weekday prayers, and others for Shabbat and holidays. The word *siddur* is related to the Hebrew word for "order." What do you think is the connection between the Jewish prayer book and order?

The Psalms: A Poem for Every Occasion

When we pray, we may be helped by the words of the great musician and poet, King David. According to Jewish tradition, King David wrote much of the Book of Psalms, a collection of 150 poems. Psalms are used throughout the siddur, especially when we want to praise God. Many are sung or set to music, making their messages even more meaningful. King David turned to God at both the high and low points of his life.

> **When I thought my foot was slipping, your kindness, O God, gave me support. . . . Adonai is my stronghold, God is my sheltering rock.** (Psalm 94:18-22)

Why do you think King David found these words comforting?

_____

_____

What words—or music—might you use to express your feelings in a poem or prayer?

_____

Your Turn

Music is an important part of prayer. Describe a piece of music, with or without lyrics, that you think would work as a prayer. Make a list of songs you would include on a personal prayer CD or playlist, and give the list a title. You can use real song titles or make up your own.

Meet Saadya

Saadya gets excited about both the Torah and his music. He sings in a Jewish choir, which enriches his Jewish community and deepens his appreciation for Jewish texts.

What I like best about being Jewish: On Shabbat, I like reading books and playing long games with my family.

My music: I've been playing the piano for three years. Sometimes my fingers are slippery and I get annoyed, but I feel like a leader when my fingers are into it and I can play anything. I am in a Jewish choir, and we had three concerts this year. I feel under pressure when singing a solo, but I am good at timing and know how to sing in rhythm, and I didn't make any mistakes. We sing songs from the siddur and holiday songs.

Music in my Jewish life: I lead some prayers in my synagogue. I switch off singing Yigdal on Friday nights with a friend, and on Shabbat mornings I usually sing Adon Olam. Learning Jewish songs from the siddur for choir helps me a lot when praying. Also, if I know the words already because I studied them, it makes it easier to learn the song and the new tunes.

Praise, Requests, and Thanks

If you were to have an audience with a king or queen or have a chance to talk to a president or another state leader, how would you prepare your words? What would you say first? How would you phrase your requests? Jewish prayer refers to God as royalty, as a ruler who deserves our praise and who can grant our wishes. Prayers are written with this in mind, and even the order of the prayers in the siddur reflects this. Generally, we first say prayers of praise to God that show our appreciation for the world we live in, then we request things that we want, and finally, we give thanks.

When I Wake Up, I Give Praise For . . .

The siddur offers blessings to be said when we start the day. By praising God for all the things we are able to do each morning, we come to appreciate things we might otherwise take for granted.

The first blessing offers appreciation for just waking up:

> **Praised are You, Adonai our God, Ruler of the universe, who gives the mind understanding to distinguish between day and night.**

For each blessing topic below, write in an activity you do in the morning. Then add your own blessings for things you are grateful for in the morning. One example is filled in for you.

I give praise to God . . .

who gives sight to the blind,   when I _first open my eyes in the morning_ .

who clothes the naked,   when I _____ .

who guides our steps,   when I _____ .

who gives Am Yisrael strength,   when I _____ .

who removes sleep from my eyes,   when I _____ .

who _____ ,   when I _____ .

who _____ ,   when I _____ .

Notes to God

The central prayer of every service is the Amidah, the "Standing Prayer," which refers to a series of blessings we say while standing. Here is where we take the opportunity to ask for the things we want, for ourselves and our family, for all of Am Yisrael, and for the whole world. Requests are the focus of the Amidah on weekdays, but no requests are made on Shabbat. Why do you think that is?

Fill in your own personal prayer for each of the topics below, found in the Amidah. Which prayers are the most important to you?

Talk about It

Why do you think we say organized prayers together as a community, in addition to any personal prayers we might say?

A prayer for . . .

Forgiveness
What is something you regret doing?

Knowledge
What would you like to learn more about?

A productive year
What would you like to accomplish this year?

The sick
Write your hopes for someone who is unwell.

Jerusalem
Write a prayer for Israel.

Justice
What problems in the world would you like to see fixed?

Moments Big and Small

The first Israeli astronaut, Ilan Ramon, said the Sh'ma when he saw Jerusalem from space. Think about an occasion in your life when you felt wonder or gratitude. Search the siddur for a prayer that helps you express those feelings, or write your own prayer of thanks for that experience.

_____

_____

Ilan Ramon

CHAPTER 8

PASS IT ON: BEING PEOPLE OF THE BOOK

"Make books your companions. Let your shelves be your treasure grounds."

(Judah ben Saul ibn Tibbon, twelfth-century Spanish translator and physician)

How have our sacred texts shaped your Jewish life? Think about all the building blocks for Jewish life contained in them—our history and stories, our language, traditions, laws, symbols, art, and values. How will you pass along your Jewish way of life to future generations?

Debate It

The sages placed great value on Torah study but also stressed doing the commandments, the mitzvot. The Talmud tells of the following debate:

Rabbi Tarfon and the Elders were . . . in Lydda, when this question was raised before them:
Is study greater, or is action greater?
Rabbi Tarfon answered, saying: Action is greater.
Rabbi Akiva answered, saying: Study is greater.
Then they all answered and said: Study is greater, for it leads to action. (Talmud, *Kiddushin* 40b)

Circle the opinion with which you agree and explain your choice:

_____

Checklist

Give yourself a big check mark for each of the Your Turn experiences you have tried.

- [ ] Plan out a biblical TV miniseries, page 18
- [ ] Write a letter or blog entry about a Torah reading or celebration, page 23
- [ ] Make a double-sided mask to explore your Jewish identity, page 27
- [ ] Create a visual midrash to depict King David, page 35
- [ ] Write a Torah commentary, page 40
- [ ] Compile a personal prayer CD or playlist, page 43

What other Jewish experiences have you tried for the first time this year?

✔ _____

✔ _____

✔ _____

Join the Book Club

Our sacred and secular books are a constant part of Jewish life. Some people read them to learn what Jewish heroes and heroines have to say, others pick them up for guidance or are drawn to inspiring tales, and some are deeply moved by the history of Am Yisrael. What role do Jewish books have in your life? Take this quiz to find out.

What is your Jewish book personality?

1. If you could meet a character from a Jewish story, who would it be?
   a. Aaron, Moses's older brother, who helped Moses lead Am Yisrael and had a peaceful manner.
   b. Beruryah, quoted in the Talmud for her wise and insightful explanations.
   c. Judah the Maccabee, the brave hero of Ḥanukkah history, who led a revolt against King Antiochus and liberated the Temple.
   d. Rebecca, the matriarch of Am Yisrael, and kind and generous mother of Jacob and Esau.

2. You are in a Jewish book club. It's your turn to pick a book. Which one sounds best to you?
   a. A biography of a Jewish leader.
   b. A book of Jewish mysteries to solve.
   c. A book that tells the story of Jewish American soldiers who held a seder during a war.
   d. An account of a Jewish family's escape from danger in their country and arrival in America.

3. What sacred Jewish book would you want to have if you were stranded on a desert island?
   a. A Tanakh, because its characters would entertain and inspire you.
   b. The *Shulḥan Aruch*, because it could help you lead a Jewish life.
   c. The Talmud, because it would help you remember Jewish law.
   d. A siddur, because you may want to pray for help.

4. Which book in Tanakh would you recommend to a president or prime minister?
   a. Exodus, so he or she can learn from the struggles and triumphs of Moses, Aaron, and Miriam.
   b. Proverbs, so he or she can be reminded of the true values in life.
   c. Samuel, so he or she can study the ways that Jewish judges, prophets, and kings rule.
   d. Megillat Esther, so he or she can see how leaders defended their nation in a time of great danger.

If you answered . . .
   Mostly a's: Lover of ideas—you like to learn about Jewish personalities and their thoughts.
   Mostly b's: Seeker of wisdom—you always have a question and thirst for more knowledge.
   Mostly c's: Defender of the law—you stand up for the Jewish religion and justice.
   Mostly d's: Protector of the Jewish nation—you care deeply about the fate of Am Yisrael.

Does this sound like you? How would you describe your Jewish book personality in your own words?

_____

_____

WORDS TO KNOW

Aliyah Hebrew for "going up;" the honor of being called up to the Torah to recite blessings before and after the reading of each section of the Torah portion *(parashah)*. To "make *aliyah*" means to move to Israel.

Chumash From the Hebrew *chameish*, meaning "five;" the Torah, or Five Books of Moses, in printed form.

Haftarah The selection from the Prophets *(Nevi'im)* read after the Torah portion *(parashah)*.

Halachah Jewish law and observances.

Megillah Hebrew for "scroll" (plural: *megillot*). Writings *(K'tuvim)* contains five scrolls: Song of Songs, Ruth, Lamentations, Ecclesiastes, and Esther (the Purim story).

Midrash Hebrew for "investigation" or "search" (plural: *midrashim*); interpretations of the Torah's stories and laws by the sages and others.

Minyan A gathering of at least ten Jewish adults for prayer or Torah reading.

Parashah Hebrew for "portion;" a section of the Torah. The Torah is divided into weekly portions to be read in synagogue. On the holiday of Simḥat Torah, we read the last *parashah* of the Torah and begin the cycle again, each week reading the next portion in order.

Siddur From the Hebrew *seder*, meaning "order;" the Jewish prayer book (plural: *siddurim*).

Talmud The written version of the Oral Law, the collected wisdom of generations of scholarly discussion about the Torah. The Talmud includes the **Mishnah**, compiled around 200 CE; the **Gemara**, the commentary and discussion on the Mishnah; and additional commentaries by Rashi and others.

Tanakh Hebrew acronym for the three parts of the Jewish Bible: Torah (the Five Books of Moses), *Nevi'im* (the Prophets), and *K'tuvim* (the Writings).

A megillah containing the Book of Esther, set in an olive wood case